From a Witch's Kitchen

Celebrating Seasonal Magic in Every Meal

By Beth Brown

Copyright © 2007 by Beth Brown

All rights reserved, including the right of
reproduction in whole or in part in any form.

For information about special discounts for bulk purchases,
please contact the author directly at:

www.Beth-Brown.com

Cover design by Beth Brown

ISBN: 978-0-6151-8570-5

Dedication

To my Mother, Grandmothers, and Great Grandmothers for taking the time to pass down the kitchen traditions in which I can now see the magic woven throughout. I only hope that I can make you all proud by adding some of my own creations to the cauldron of family treasures you've left behind.

Contents

Introduction	7
Winter's Comforts	9
Spring's Awakening	31
Summer's Bounty	49
Autumn's Folly	75
Cook's Notes	93
Index	97

Introduction

Welcome. If you've picked up this book then you're obviously interested in at least one of two things: witchcraft or cooking. In my mind, the two go hand in hand. When you stop to think about it, how is a recipe that heals, comforts, refreshes, or invigorates any different from a spell?

Anyone can pop a frozen meal into the oven or microwave. What they're lacking is the fulfillment that comes from touching the ingredients with your own hands, incorporating the love and attention of each carefully selected addition, and the true magic that is stirred into every meal by those that tend to the process. No one can deny that a home-cooked meal tastes exponentially better than a factory processed one. It all comes down to the power that pours out of the person doing the cooking and keeping the hearth.

I make no reference to deities or higher powers in these pages as I believe that those you prefer to honor and elevate are yours to choose individually and without my influence. Then how can I call this a "witches' cookbook" if I refer to no Pagan gods or goddesses? I've decided to write recipes that evoke the country witches of the past who spent countless days observing and connecting with the cycles of the land and sky around them. The only thing I've elevated in this book are the various edible gifts from the earth at their naturally occurring peak. I encourage you to speak from the heart and give thanks for those gifts to whom you see fit. There are no rituals or spells in this book. I have experienced first-hand that the most powerful rituals and spells are those that *you* craft for your individual purpose using your instincts. I hope that you will use the recipes here to ground yourself and to inspire your own spell-writing.

What I want to share with you in this book is an appreciation of foods from each season and the different types of magical energy we draw from our meals throughout the year. Celebrating the Earth and her cycle of life is a tradition rooted deep in all of us – I want you to get to the kitchen and bring a celebration to every plate!

Winter's Comforts

    The gray skies of winter and the long, cold nights leave our souls and bodies hungry for something warm and comforting. Now is the time to spend the evenings in front of a warm oven or bubbling pot while you reflect on all of the things that bring you warm and happy emotions. I love to stir a huge kettle of soup or stew while thinking about the delicious smells that would fill the house and the musical clanking that came from the kitchen when my grandmother would spend a Sunday tending to hers.

    Comfort of the soul comes in many different forms to different people. Some don't feel their house is a home in Winter without the spicy scent of cinnamon or clove. Others only long to cozy up to the fireplace to daydream and rejuvenate. A hot mug of cider or cocoa on a chilly day does double duty as a soul soother and a treat for the physical body. Finding your personal comforts this Winter and celebrating and embracing them is the best place to start building your magical traditions and ties with the season.

    While preparing some of the following dishes, let your mind wander and reflect on comforting memories of the Winter kitchen. Take some time to honor your ancestors and to appreciate all of the hardships that this dark season meant to those long ago.

    Winter's element is Earth - ground yourself and allow your mind to open to the things that bring you comfort. This is a time when root vegetables prevail in the kitchen and rich, wholesome recipes fill you and your family with the warmth of the hearth.

Mulled Cider
Serves 10-12

Warm ginger ale adds an unexpected flavor as well as frugality to this warm drink.

> 2 quarts apple cider
> 1 quart ginger ale
> juice of 2 lemons
> 1 cup diced dried apples
> ½ cup brown sugar
> ½ tsp. whole allspice
> 1 tsp. whole cloves
> 2 cinnamon sticks
> ¼ tsp. ground nutmeg

Combine all ingredients in a large saucepan and bring to a boil. Reduce heat and allow to simmer for 15 minutes, stirring occasionally. Remove from heat and strain off the spices through a coffee filter or fine sieve. Serve hot.

Mulled Wine
Serves 4-6

This recipe is simple enough to prepare for a small group or to double for a large crowd. It truly warms you from the inside out!

- **2 bottles dry red wine**
- **2 Tbsp. sugar**
- **2 cinnamon sticks**
- **6 whole cloves**
- **1 Tbsp. grated lemon peel**
- **2 Tbsp. cognac or rum**

Combine wine and sugar in a large saucepan. Add cinnamon, cloves, and lemon peel. Heat, without boiling, to dissolve sugar. Remove from heat and add cognac or rum. Let the mixture sit for 10 minutes to allow the flavors to develop. Strain off the spices through a coffee filter or a fine sieve. Serve hot.

Deluxe Hot Chocolate
Serves 4-6

Remember cupping your hands around a warm mug of hot cocoa as a child? Bring back that simple pleasure with this delicious grown-up version.

3 ¼ cups milk
¾ cup heavy cream
1 ½ tsp. pure vanilla extract
6 oz. bittersweet chocolate, chopped

Combine milk, cream, and vanilla in a saucepan and scald over low heat. In a bowl, mix the chocolate and about ¾ cup of the warmed milk mixture, whisking until the chocolate is smooth and melted. Add the chocolate mixture to the remaining milk and simmer, whisking, until thoroughly heated but not boiling. Serve hot and, if you wish, topped with a dollop of whipped cream.

Warm and Sunny Carrot Soup
Serves 4-6

Spicy ginger brings a surprising flavor to this bright and cheerful soup. My family loves this served with a pat of butter on top and a piece of crusty bread.

    3 lbs. carrots, cut into 1-inch chunks
    water to cover
    2 Tbsp. sugar
    2 Tbsp. finely diced fresh gingerroot
    1 tsp. salt

In a Dutch oven or other large pot, combine carrots, diced ginger, and water. Cover and boil until carrots are tender. Drain, reserving about 1-2 cups of the cooking water. Transfer half of the carrot and ginger mixture to a blender and add about ½ cup of the cooking water. Puree until smooth. Pour carrot puree into a large pot. Repeat the process with the second half of the carrots. Add reserved cooking water to the puree until the soup is the thickness of heavy cream or slightly thicker, depending on your preference. Stir in salt and sugar. Serve hot.

Making this soup one day ahead allows the ginger flavor to fully develop and gives the dish a warming effect. Try it topped with a sprinkle of ground cinnamon for an added treat.

Creamy Potato and Onion Soup
Serves 4-6

The wholesome and filling potato meets the comfort of warm milk. Again, this is a fantastic soup to serve with crusty bread for dipping.

4 lbs. potatoes, peeled and cut into 1-inch chunks
water to cover
2 large onions, finely diced
1 ½ cups half-and-half or heavy cream
2 Tbsp. olive oil
2 tsp. salt
coarsely ground black pepper, to taste

In a large pot, combine potatoes, water, and salt. Cover and boil until the potatoes are just fork tender. Drain off about 1/3 of the cooking water.

In a skillet, sauté onions in olive oil at medium heat until golden brown. Add onions to potatoes and remaining cooking water. Stir in half-and-half or heavy cream. Season with black pepper to taste. Simmer uncovered, stirring frequently, until potatoes are soft and soup thickens slightly. Serve hot.

Black Bean, Rice, and Chipotle Stew
Serves 4-6

Spicy chipotle chiles add warmth to traditional (and filling) black beans and rice.

> 1 bay leaf
> 1 cup onion, finely chopped
> 2 celery stalks, finely chopped
> 2 canned chipotle peppers, minced
> 1 cup frozen white corn kernels
> 2 Tbsp. olive oil
> 3 cloves garlic, chopped
> 2 15-oz. cans black beans
> 2 tsp. chili powder
> 1 32-oz. carton vegetable stock
> 1 15-oz. can diced tomatoes
> 1 tsp. ground coriander
> 1½ tsp. cumin
> 1 8-oz. can tomato sauce
> 1 cup long-grain white rice

Combine all ingredients except rice in a large soup kettle. Bring to a slow boil, reduce heat and cover. Allow stew to simmer for about 30 minutes. Stir in rice, cover, and continue to simmer until rice is tender, about 10 to 15 minutes. Spoon into bowls and top with a pinch of shredded cheese or a dollop of sour cream, if desired. Serve hot.

Quick and Creamy Curry
Serves 4-6

Exotic spices and hearty vegetables combine to create this satisfying one-pot meal.

> 2 cups peeled and cubed potatoes
> 2 cups carrots, cut into 1-inch chunks
> 2 cups frozen cauliflower pieces
> 2 cups frozen cut green beans
> 3 cups water or low-sodium vegetable broth
> 2 large onions, diced
> 1 cup plain yogurt
> 1 cup sour cream
> 3 Tbsp. vegetable oil
> 3 Tbsp. curry powder
> 2 Tbsp. sugar
> 1 ½ tsp. salt

Heat oil in a large pot. Stir in onions and sauté over medium heat until translucent. Add curry powder and stir constantly for about 20 seconds; quickly add water or broth and bring to a boil. Add vegetables and salt. Cover and simmer on low heat until carrots and potatoes are fork tender (about ten to fifteen minutes.) Remove from heat and stir in yogurt, sour cream, and sugar. Serve over prepared Basmati rice or with warmed flatbread.

Winter Potato Salad with Snow Peas

Serves 4-6

Here is a Summer favorite adapted for Winter comfort.

>6 medium potatoes, well scrubbed
>1 cup snow peas, trimmed and steamed until tender
>1 small zucchini, quartered and thinly sliced
>3 Tbsp. fresh parsley, minced
>¼ cup olive oil
>¼ cup red wine vinegar
>½ tsp. Dijon mustard
>1 tsp. dried dill weed
>2 green onions, both green and white parts, chopped
>salt and pepper to taste

Boil the potatoes, unpeeled, until they are just fork tender. Cool to room temperature and cut them in half lengthwise and then into 1/2-inch slices. Whisk remaining ingredients together in a large mixing bowl until thoroughly blended. Add potato slices and toss to coat. Serve at room temperature.

Nutty Brown Rice Salad
Serves 4-6

This toasty recipe will quickly become a requested favorite at all of the season's annual get-togethers.

> 1 cup brown rice
> 1 cup chopped nuts (your choice of almonds, walnuts, cashews, or any combination)
> 1 green onion, finely chopped
> 1 large green pepper, seeded and finely chopped
> 1 Tbsp. soy sauce
> 3 Tbsp. lemon juice
> ½ tsp. ground cumin
> 2 tsp. Dijon mustard
> ¾ cup mayonnaise
> pepper to taste

Cook the rice according to its package directions. Allow it to cool to room temperature.

In a dry skillet over medium heat, toast the nuts, stirring constantly, until just golden and fragrant. Remove from pan and allow to cool on a plate.

In a large mixing bowl, whisk together lemon juice, soy sauce, Dijon mustard, and mayonnaise. Add remaining ingredients, including rice and nuts, and stir thoroughly. Add freshly ground pepper to taste. Serve warm or cool.

Butternut Squash and Hazelnut Lasagna
Serves 4-6

This rich and cheesy dish demands center stage! Its golden color celebrates the return of the sun and its delicate flavor is perfect for any Winter potluck or special family dinner.

For the Squash Filling
3 lb. butternut squash, peeled, seeded, and cut into 1/2-inch pieces
1 large onion, chopped
3 Tbsp. unsalted butter
1 tsp. minced garlic
1 tsp. salt
1/4 tsp. white pepper
2 Tbsp. chopped fresh flat-leaf parsley
4 tsp. chopped fresh sage
1 cup hazelnuts (4 oz), toasted, loose skins rubbed off with a kitchen towel, and coarsely chopped

For the Sauce
1 tsp. minced garlic
3 Tbsp. unsalted butter
5 Tbsp. all-purpose flour
5 cups milk
1 bay leaf
1 tsp. salt
1/8 tsp. white pepper

For Assembling the Lasagna
2 cups shredded mozzarella
1 cup finely grated Parmesan cheese
12 (7- by 3 1/2-inch) sheets no-boil lasagna

Make filling:
Heat butter in a heavy skillet and sauté onion until golden brown. Add squash, garlic, salt, and white pepper and cover to cook, stirring occasionally, until squash is just tender. Remove from heat and stir in parsley, sage, and nuts. Allow to cool.

Make sauce while squash cooks:
In a saucepan, lightly sauté garlic in butter. Whisk in flour and cook roux, stirring constantly, for about two minutes. Slowly whisk in milk. Add bay leaf and bring to a low boil, whisking constantly. Reduce heat and simmer, whisking occasionally, 10 minutes. Stir in salt and white pepper and remove from heat. Discard bay leaf. (Cover surface of sauce with wax paper if not using immediately to prevent a skin from forming.)

Assemble lasagna:
Preheat oven to 425°F. Toss cheeses together. Spread 1/2 cup sauce in a buttered 13- by 9- by 2-inch glass baking dish and cover with 3 pasta sheets, leaving spaces between sheets. Spread with 2/3 cup sauce and one third of filling, and then sprinkle with a heaping 1/2 cup cheese. Repeat layering 2 more times, beginning with pasta sheets and ending with cheese. Top with remaining 3 pasta sheets, remaining sauce, and remaining cheese.

Tightly cover baking dish with buttered foil and bake lasagna in middle of oven 30 minutes. Remove foil and bake until golden and bubbling, 10 to 15 minutes more. Allow lasagna stand 15 to 20 minutes before serving.

Chestnut Risotto with Butternut Squash
Serves 4-6

Always-comforting risotto pairs amazingly well with the sweetness of butternut squash. Chestnuts are a special highlight of the Winter menu and help balance the flavors of this one-dish supper.

> 6 cups low-salt vegetable broth
> ¼ cup cream Sherry
> 1 Tbsp. olive oil
> 3 Tbsp. butter, divided
> 1 small white onion, finely chopped
> ½ small butternut squash, peeled, seeded, cut into 1/4-inch pieces
> 1 ½ cups (10 ounces) Arborio rice
> 2 cups peeled roasted chestnuts, or jarred chestnuts, chopped
> 1 tsp. chopped fresh thyme
> 1 tsp. chopped fresh marjoram
> ½ cup freshly grated Parmesan cheese
> 2 Tbsp. chopped fresh Italian parsley

Bring broth and Sherry to boil in medium saucepan over high heat. Reduce heat to low; cover and keep warm.

Heat oil and 2 tablespoons butter in a large saucepan over medium heat. Add onion and squash; cook until onion is translucent. Add rice; stir until rice is translucent at edges but still opaque in center, about 3 minutes. Add 1 cup warm broth; simmer until almost absorbed, stirring often, about 4 minutes. Add more broth, 1 cup at a time, allowing each addition to be absorbed before adding next until rice is just tender, stirring frequently, about 25 minutes total. Stir in chestnuts, thyme, and marjoram. Remove from heat; stir in remaining 1 tablespoon butter, cheese, and parsley.

Season risotto with salt and pepper to taste. Serve hot.

Shepherd's Pie with Potato Topping
Serves 6-10

This classic British dish is my ideal comfort food. It is easier than it sounds to prepare because, even though it is called a pie, there is no pastry involved.

> 3 ½ pounds russet potatoes, peeled and cut into 2-inch pieces
> 1 cup vegetable broth
> 2 tsp. Dijon mustard
> ½ tsp salt
> black pepper to taste
>
> 3 medium carrots, peeled and diced into ½-inch pieces
> 1 medium onion, finely chopped
> 3 cloves garlic, finely chopped
> 1 ½ lbs. ground beef style soy "crumbles"
> 1 cup thawed frozen peas
> ¾ cup thawed frozen corn kernels
> 1 14-oz. can diced tomatoes, drained
> 1 Tbsp. tomato paste
> salt and pepper to taste

In a large saucepan, combine potatoes with enough water to cover by about 1 inch. Bring to a boil and cook until very tender, about 15 minutes. Drain well. In a large mixing bowl, combine potatoes, broth, mustard, salt, and pepper to taste. Use an electric mixer and beat until smooth. Set aside.

Preheat oven to 350°F. In a small saucepan, boil carrots for about 2 minutes to blanch. Drain and set aside.

In a large non-stick skillet, sauté the onion over low heat until translucent, about 2 minutes. Add the garlic, soy crumbles, blanched carrots, peas, corn, tomatoes, and tomato paste. Mix well and cool for about 10 minutes to allow the flavors to meld. Season with salt and pepper to taste.

Lightly oil a 3-quart casserole dish and spoon in the prepared vegetable and soy crumble mixture. Top with dollops of mashed potatoes. Bake for 30 to 45 minutes or until heated through. Serve hot.

Cheddar and Cider Fondue
Serves 4-6

Legend has it that fondue was created out of necessity during an especially long and harsh winter. When the stored meats were depleted and the preserved vegetables gone, folks were left to get creative with the flour and cheeses that were remaining. My version is non-alcoholic and zesty.

> 1 cup Apple Cider (to mix with cheese)
> ¼ cup Apple Cider (to mix with cornstarch & mustard)
> 3 tsp. Lemon Juice
> 1 Tbsp. onion, finely chopped
> 3 cups shredded Cheddar Cheese
> 1 Tbsp. cornstarch
> 2/3 tsp. mustard powder
> white pepper to taste

In a medium saucepan over low heat, warm the cider, lemon juice & onion. Cook, stirring occasionally, for about 15 minutes to allow the flavors to meld. Slowly stir in cheese, about one cup at a time. Mix cornstarch and mustard in 1/4 cup apple cider and stir until lumps are dissolved. Stir the cornstarch mixture into the cheese and continue to cook for about one minute. Remove from heat and add white pepper to taste. Use your choice of cubed bread for dipping. Serve warm.

Dried Fruit Pudding
Serves 4-6

Dry preserved fruits from Summer's crop keep well in tightly sealed jars. Showcase your bounty in this hot bread pudding similar to Apple Brown Betty. It makes a great dessert, breakfast, or brunch selection!

1 cup brown sugar
½ tsp. ground cinnamon
¼ tsp. ground nutmeg
¼ tsp. ground cloves
¼ tsp. salt
2 cups stale bread, cut into small cubes or crumbled
2 cups mixed dried fruits such as raisins, currants, cranberries, apples, and apricots
½ cup orange juice
4 Tbsp. butter

Preheat oven to 350° F. Blend sugar, spices, and salt together in a small bowl. Arrange 1/3 of the crumbled or cubed bread in a greased 2-quart baking dish. Add ½ of the fruit mixture. Sprinkle fruit with ½ of the sugar and spice blend. Repeat the process, finishing with a layer of bread. Pour orange juice evenly over the layers and dot the top with bits of butter. Cover with foil and bake for about 30 minutes. Remove foil and bake an additional 15 minutes until the top is golden brown. Serve warm.

Golden Sun Rum Cake
Serves 8-10

This golden cake celebrates the return of longer days and shorter nights. Using a cake mix makes it quick and easy and the sticky, sweet butter rum glaze makes it a wonderful treat for special occasions.

For the cake:
1 cup chopped pecans
1 (18.25 oz.) package yellow cake mix
4 eggs
½ cup water
½ cup vegetable oil
½ cup dark rum

For the glaze:
1 cup brown sugar
½ cup butter
½ cup dark rum
¼ cup water

Preheat oven to 325° F. Grease and flour a 10-inch Bundt pan. Sprinkle chopped pecans even around the bottom of pan.

In a large bowl, combine cake mix, eggs, ½ cup water, oil, and ½ cup rum. Mix well and pour batter into the pan over the chopped pecans. Bake for about one hour, or until a toothpick inserted into the cake comes out clean. Allow cake to cool for about 10 minutes in the pan and then turn it out onto a plate.

In a saucepan, combine butter, ¼ cup water, and brown sugar. Bring to a boil over medium heat and continue to boil for 2-3 minutes, stirring constantly. Remove from heat and stir in ½ cup rum.

A clean and easy method of glazing your cake is to pour ½ of glaze mixture into the Bundt pan and return the cake to the pan to absorb the glaze. Thoroughly pierce the bottom of the cake with a toothpick and top with remaining ½ of glaze. Allow the cake to rest in the pan for about 20 minutes, or until most of the mixture has been absorbed, and turn it out onto a serving platter.

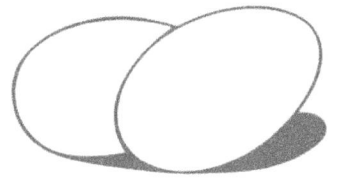

Spring's Awakening

The first flowers have started peeking out from the snow and the trees are sporting soft, tiny buds. By this time, you'll likely notice a feeling of renewal and increased energy in your own body, too. Winter's gray skies are lifting and the invigorating spring air is waking the world.

Gardens are being freshly dug and, in what seems like only a matter of days, the first tender young vegetables will make a welcome appearance. Symbols of fertility abound – peas and seeds, sprouts, and eggs are some of the most easy to recognize. Celebrate their return by making them the focus of each meal instead of a tiny side dish. With each plate this season, imagine yourself absorbing Spring's revitalizing energy and let your body enjoy every invigorating bite!

Spring's element is water – now is the time to open your windows on a warm day and pull out a pail of herb-infused water to wash away all of Winter's heaviness.

Thyme and Mint Infusion
Serves 4-6

Light and flavorful herbs help to awaken the taste buds after a long winter's nap.

2 tsp. dried thyme
2 Tbsp. fresh mint leaves, crushed or bruised
3 Tbsp. honey
6 cups water

Bring the water to a rolling boil in either a saucepan or tea kettle. Remove from heat and stir in herbs and honey. Allow the mixture to steep for about 4 or 5 minutes. Strain off the herbs using a coffee filter or a fine sieve and transfer infusion to cups. Serve warm or iced.

Lemon Ginger Infusion
Serves 4

This soothing and aromatic infusion is great for relieving stress and also a good remedy for Spring allergies.

1 small lemon, thinly sliced
1 Tbsp. fresh gingerroot, peeled and finely chopped
4 Tbsp. honey
4 cups water

Bring the water to a rolling boil in either a saucepan or tea kettle. Remove from heat and stir in lemon, ginger, and honey. Allow the mixture to steep for about 10 minutes. Strain off the herbs using a coffee filter or a fine sieve and transfer infusion to cups. Serve warm.

Lavender, Mint, and Lemon Infusion
Serves 4

Don't let the addition of flowers discourage you from trying this restorative treat! Lavender adds a soothing quality to the stimulating flavors of mint and lemon and truly balances this beverage.

> 1 small lemon, thinly sliced
> 2 Tbsp. fresh mint leaves, crushed or bruised
> 1 Tbsp. dried lavender flowers (available at most spice shops and natural food stores)
> 2 Tbsp. honey
> 4 cups water

Bring the water to a rolling boil in either a saucepan or tea kettle. Remove from heat and stir in lemon, mint, lavender flowers, and honey. Allow the mixture to steep for about 10 minutes. Strain off the herbs using a coffee filter or a fine sieve and transfer infusion to cups. Serve warm.

Lentil Soup with Spinach
Serves 6-8

The lively flavors of mint and oregano add a surprising touch to this beautiful Spring soup.

> 2 Tbsp. olive oil
> 2 cups chopped onion
> ½ cup chopped celery, with leaves
> 2 cloves garlic, finely minced
> 8 cups water
> 3 ½ cups vegetable broth
> 2 ½ cups dried lentils, sorted and rinsed
> 1 16-oz. can diced tomatoes, undrained
> 1 ½ tsp. salt
> ½ tsp freshly ground black pepper
> 1 Tbsp. chopped fresh mint leaves (or 1 tsp. dried)
> 1 Tbsp. chopped fresh oregano leaves (or 1 tsp. dried)
> 1 10-oz package fresh baby spinach leaves

Heat the olive oil in a large pot over medium heat. Add the onion, celery, and garlic and cook until softened, about 8 minutes. Add the water, broth, and lentils. Bring to a boil over high heat. Reduce heat to low, cover, and simmer for about 1 hour, or until the lentils are tender.

Add the tomatoes and their juice to the pot. Stir in salt, pepper, mint, and oregano. Bring to a boil over medium heat. Reduce heat to low and allow to simmer, uncovered, for 5 minutes. Add the spinach and allow to simmer an additional 5 minutes. Serve hot.

Pea Salad with Radishes and Feta Cheese
Serves 4-6

This fresh salad incorporates many of Spring's best flavors in one dish and offers a welcome reprieve from Winter's heavy soups and stews.

> 2 tsp. cumin seeds
> 2 Tbsp. fresh lime juice
> 2 tsp. honey
> ¼ cup extra-virgin olive oil
> 3 Tbsp. chopped fresh dill
>
> 4 cups fresh shelled peas (from about 4 pounds peas in pods) or 1 pound frozen petite peas
> 1 bunch radishes, trimmed, halved, thinly sliced
> 1 cup crumbled feta cheese (about 4 ounces)
> 3 cups fresh pea sprouts

Toast cumin seeds in a small, dry skillet until aromatic and slightly darker, about 2 minutes. Cool; grind finely in spice mill or with a mortar and pestle. Whisk lime juice, honey, and cumin in small bowl. Gradually whisk in oil; stir in dill. Season dressing mixture to taste with salt and pepper.

Cook peas in pot of boiling salted water until almost tender, about 5 minutes for fresh (or about 2 minutes for frozen). Drain; rinse under cold water, then drain well. Transfer to large bowl. Add radishes, feta, and dressing; toss. Season with salt and pepper. Divide pea sprouts evenly among serving plates or bowls and top with the salad mixture. Serve cool.

Mediterranean Couscous Salad
Serves 4-6

Family and guests alike will adore the lightness and fluffiness of this salad paired with the fresh, herbal bite of green onion and basil.

2 ¼ cups vegetable broth
10 oz. couscous (about 1 ¼ cups)
1 cup finely chopped green onion, both the white and light green parts
1 cup diced plum or Roma tomatoes
1/3 cup thinly sliced fresh basil
½ cup extra-virgin olive oil
¼ cup balsamic vinegar
¼ tsp red pepper flakes
salt and pepper to taste

Bring the broth to a boil in a medium saucepan. Stir in the couscous; remove from heat, cover, and let stand for 5 minutes. Fluff couscous with a fork and allow it to cool.

Add the green onion, tomatoes, basil, olive oil, vinegar, and red pepper flakes to the couscous and toss to mix. Season the mixture to taste with salt and pepper. Serve at room temperature or slightly chilled.

Easy Lemon Dill Egg Salad
Serves 6-8

This is a twist on traditional egg salad that is perfect for picnics and potluck suppers. Serve on toast, Kaiser buns, or in pitas with fresh sprouts.

> 6 eggs
> 2 green onions, finely chopped
> 1 stalk celery, chopped
> ½ cup red bell pepper, chopped
> ½ tsp. lemon pepper seasoning
> 1 tsp. dried dill weed
> ¾ cup prepared ranch salad dressing

Add eggs to a medium saucepan and cover with cool water by about 1 ½ inches. Bring to a rolling boil, partly covered, and remove from heat after about 45 seconds. Allow eggs to rest in the covered pan for about 15 minutes. Drain pan and rinse eggs under cold water for 2 to 3 minutes to stop the cooking. Peel and chop cooled eggs.

In a large bowl, combine remaining ingredients with chopped eggs and stir to coat. Cover mixture with a tight-fitting lid or plastic wrap and allow it to chill for at least one hour. Serve cold.

Hummus Pita Sandwiches
Serves 4

Making the hummus a day or so ahead allows the rich, garlicky flavor to fully develop.

> 2 Tbsp. sesame seeds
> 1 15-oz. can chickpeas (garbanzo beans)
> 2 cloves garlic
> ¼ cup loosely packed parsley sprigs
> 3 Tbsp. lemon juice
> 1 Tbsp. olive oil
> 4 pita bread rounds
> 2 tomatoes, thinly sliced
> 1 cucumber, thinly sliced
> 1 cup alfalfa sprouts, rinsed and drained
> 2 Tbsp. crumbled feta cheese

Toast sesame seeds in a small non-stick skillet over medium heat until lightly browned, tossing frequently. Remove from skillet and allow to cool.

Drain chickpeas, reserving the liquid. Place chickpeas, garlic, parsley, lemon juice, and olive oil in a food processor and process until smooth, scraping sides of bowl once. If mixture is very thick, add 1 to 2 tablespoons of reserved chickpea liquid and process to blend. Spoon hummus mixture into a medium bowl and stir in sesame seeds.

Cut pita breads in half. Spread about 3 tablespoons of hummus into each half. Divide tomatoes, cucumber, and sprouts evenly and add to pitas. Sprinkle with feta cheese and serve.

Moroccan Potato and Egg Sandwiches
Serves 4

Try these delicious sandwiches with a sprinkle of cayenne pepper for a kick!

> 4 large eggs
> 2 tsp. ground cumin
> 2 green peppers, seeded and cut into thin strips
> 1 large onion, thinly sliced
> 3/4 lb boiling potatoes, peeled and thinly sliced
> 1/2 teaspoon salt
> black pepper to taste
> 3 tablespoons extra-virgin olive oil
> 4 Kaiser rolls (about 4 inches in diameter)

Add eggs to a medium saucepan and cover with cool water by about 1 ½ inches. Bring to a rolling boil, partly covered, and remove from heat after about 45 seconds. Allow eggs to rest in the covered pan for about 15 minutes. Drain pan and rinse eggs under cold water for 2 to 3 minutes to stop the cooking. Peel eggs and cut them into quarters.

Warm oil in a large skillet over medium heat. Add onions, green peppers, potatoes, salt, and pepper. Cover and cook until vegetables are browned and very tender, about 20 minutes. Stir in cumin and toss vegetables to coat.

Scoop out a few pieces of the center of each Kaiser roll to allow room for sandwich filling. Place two egg quarters on the bottom of each roll and add a heaping scoop of the potato mixture. Finish each with two additional egg quarters and replace the top of the bun. Serve warm.

Penne with Asparagus Pesto
Serves 4-6

Fresh asparagus is one of Spring's most notable flavors. No other vegetable quite compares to this noble member of the lily family, especially during its peak season.

1 16-oz. box penne
1 lb. fresh asparagus, trimmed and cut into 2-inch pieces, tips reserved
¼ cup toasted pine nuts
2 cloves garlic, finely chopped
½ cup packed chopped fresh basil
½ cup extra-virgin olive oil
2 ½ tsp. salt, plus more to taste
1/3 cup grated Parmesan cheese
Freshly ground black pepper

Bring a large pot of salted water to a rolling boil. Add pasta and stir to prevent sticking. Cook about 8 to 10 minutes, or until al dente. Reserve 1/3 cup of the cooking water and drain the pasta well. Return penne to the pot after draining.

While pasta is cooking, steam asparagus pieces for about 4 minutes. Add the reserved tips and steam until just tender, about 1 minute. Rinse with or dip asparagus into ice water to stop the cooking and to reserve the beautiful green color. Drain well and pat dry.

Combine pine nuts, garlic, and basil in a food processor and process until finely chopped. Add the asparagus, olive oil, and salt and pulse until the asparagus is coarsely chopped. Transfer to a large bowl and stir in the Parmesan and reserved cooking water. Add penne, tossing to coat, and season to taste with salt and freshly ground pepper. Top with additional Parmesan, if desired. Serve hot.

Pad Thai
Serves 4-6

This is a very popular dish that boasts an interesting mix of textures and flavors.

> 8 oz. dried rice noodles
> ¼ cup fresh lime juice
> 2 Tbsp. tamari or low-sodium soy sauce
> 2 Tbsp. brown sugar
> 1 to 2 tsp. hot chile sauce, to taste
> 1 Tbsp. water
> 2 tsp. peanut oil
> 3 cloves garlic, finely minced
> 1 to 2 tsp. fresh ginger, peeled and finely minced
> 1 medium carrot, peeled and cut into narrow strips
> 8 to 10 green onions, halved lengthwise and cut into 2-inch pieces
> 1 cup mung bean sprouts
> 2 Tbsp. dry roasted peanuts
> ¼ cup fresh cilantro, chopped

Soak rice noodles in a large bowl of warm water, covered, until limp and white (about 20 minutes.) In a small bowl, combine lime juice, tamari, brown sugar, chile sauce, and water. Whisk well.

In a wok or large skillet, heat the oil over high heat. Add garlic and ginger and stir-fry for 20-30 seconds. Add the carrot and green onions and stir-fry for 1 minute. Stir in the sauce mixture. Drain the prepared noodles and add to the wok, tossing with tongs until softened and curled, about 1 minute. Add the sprouts and toss to mix. Transfer to serving plates and sprinkle with peanuts to garnish. Serve warm.

Mushroom and Artichoke Bake
Serves 6-8

Here is a quick and easy casserole that is perfect for a Spring picnic or potluck.

> 1 ½ cups mushrooms, sliced
> ½ cup onion, finely chopped
> 1 Tbsp. olive oil
> 2 cups cottage cheese
> 8 eggs
> ½ cup all-purpose flour
> 4 ounces crumbled feta cheese
> 1 14-oz. can artichoke hearts, rinsed, drained and chopped
> ½ cup grated Parmesan cheese

Preheat oven to 350°F. Lightly coat a 2-quart rectangular baking dish with cooking spray; set aside.

In a large skillet cook mushrooms and onion in hot olive oil until tender; set aside.

In a large bowl beat together the cottage cheese, eggs, and flour. Stir in feta cheese, artichokes, mushroom mixture and Parmesan cheese. Pour mixture into the prepared dish. Bake about 35 minutes or until a knife inserted near the center comes out clean. Serve warm.

Fig and Nutmeg Coffee Cake
Serves 10-12

This versatile treat can be served for breakfast, brunch, tea, or dessert. Though coffee cakes are sometimes seen as dull, the addition of sweet dried figs elevates this recipe to suit even the most special occasions.

1/3 cup honey
½ tsp. grated lemon peel
2 cups all-purpose flour
1 ½ tsp. ground nutmeg
1 tsp. baking powder
¼ tsp. salt
½ cup butter, softened
1 ½ cups sugar
2 eggs
1 8-ounce carton dairy sour cream
1 ½ cups snipped dried figs

Preheat oven to 350°F. Grease and lightly flour an 8- to 10-cup fluted tube pan or mold; set aside.

In a medium bowl, combine flour, nutmeg, baking powder, and salt; set aside. In a large mixing bowl beat butter with electric mixer on medium speed for 30 seconds. Add sugar; beat until combined. Add eggs, one at a time, beating well after each addition. Alternately add the flour mixture and the sour cream, beating after each addition until combined (batter will be thick). Stir in dried figs.

Spoon the batter evenly into prepared pan. Bake for 60 minutes or until toothpick inserted near center comes out clean. Cool in pan on wire rack for 10 minutes. Remove from pan. Cool on the rack for 30 minutes. Place rack over a piece of waxed paper.

Mix together honey and lemon peel and spoon over cake. Serve at room temperature or warmed for a few seconds in the microwave.

Lemon Pepper Penne Primavera

Serves 4

The refreshing bite of lemon pairs surprisingly well with dill in this light pasta dish.

> 1 16-oz box penne
> ¼ cup olive oil
> ½ cup onion, halved and thinly sliced
> 2 cloves garlic, finely minced
> ½ cup broccoli florets
> ¾ cup fresh asparagus, cut into 2-inch pieces
> ½ cup sliced mushrooms
> 1 Tbsp. lemon pepper seasoning
> ½ tsp. dried dill weed
> ¼ cup white Zinfandel wine
> ¼ cup grated Parmesan cheese

In a large pot of boiling water, add lemon pepper seasoning and pasta. Cook for 8 to 10 minutes, or according to package directions. Drain and reserve ¾ cup cooking liquid.

Meanwhile, heat olive oil in a large skillet and sauté onions until translucent. Add garlic, broccoli, asparagus, mushrooms, dill, and salt and pepper to taste. Stir-fry vegetable mixture for about 5 minutes, until all are slightly tender. Add reserved pasta cooking liquid and wine. Simmer for 3 minutes and then add hot pasta, tossing with tongs to blend.

Top with Parmesan cheese and serve hot.

Spicy Soba Noodles
Serves 4

Tender Japanese buckwheat noodles deliver a charge of the season's energy with fresh green onions and red pepper flakes.

> ½ cup soy sauce
> ½ cup light brown sugar
> ¼ cup tahini
> 2 garlic cloves, finely minced
> ½ tsp. dried red pepper flakes
> ¼ cup light sesame oil
> 6 green onions, both white and green parts, chopped
> 1 lb. dried soba noodles

In a large pot of boiling salted water, cook soba noodles until just tender, about 5 minutes. Drain.

Meanwhile, in a small saucepan, heat together the soy sauce, brown sugar, tahini, garlic, and red pepper. Whisk the mixture until the brown sugar and tahini have melted and become smooth. Stir in the sesame oil and green onions and remove from heat.

Return the noodles to their cooking pot and toss with the sauce mixture to evenly coat. Transfer to bowls and serve warm.

Summer's Bounty

Spring's flowery headiness makes its transition into Summer. Gardens overflow with plump, ripe pleasures in red, yellow, green, and even purple that we welcome to our kitchens with open arms. Gifts from the Earth are plentiful now.

One of my favorite flavors of Summer is that of a vine-ripened tomato. I add a different variety to the garden each year and enjoy experimenting with their unique tastes and textures. If you're a city dweller or novice gardener, try your hand at a single tomato plant grown in a pot or bucket on a patio. One plant can provide a surprising amount of fruit and can help you connect with the Earth and its cycles more quickly than you may expect.

Cool salads, sweet berries, melons, and bright, vibrant flavors make this season's table refreshing and festive. Leafy herbs are abundant and should be enjoyed all Summer, not just special occasions. Collect your favorites now, while they are at their peak, and hang them upside-down in a dry, dark place for use in Fall and Winter soups.

Late Summer marks the first grain harvest. Traditional agricultural festivals of this season often showcase dozens of homemade breads that truly pay tribute to the versatility of these yields. Why not try your hand at a tender loaf baked over the coals in your grill?

Summer's element is fire, symbolized by the Sun. Celebrate the power we draw from the Sun and Sky by enjoying your meals outdoors!

Lemonade with Watermelon and Basil
Serves 4-6

This unusual twist on classic lemonade has become an annual request at cookouts and Summer gatherings!

> ¼ cup fresh basil leaves
> 1 cup lemon juice (juice from 4 lemons, rinds reserved)
> ½ cup sugar
> 4 cups boiling water
> 3 cups pureed watermelon

In a very large bowl or heat-proof pitcher, bruise the basil leaves with a wooden spoon and add lemon juice and sugar. Pour boiling water over the mixture and stir until the sugar is completely dissolved. Add lemon rinds and pureed watermelon. Cover and chill for 2 to 3 hours.

Remove and discard lemon rinds. Strain the remaining mixture through coffee filters or a very fine sieve into a serving pitcher. Add a small, fresh watermelon slice and a few basil leaves to garnish. Stir well before serving and pour over ice.

Raspberry Lime Lemonade
Serves 8-10

This refreshing beverage is as lovely as it is delicious.

1 ½ cups lemon juice (from 6 large lemons)
1/3 cup lime juice (from 2 limes)
1 cup sugar
6 cups water
1 cup fresh raspberries

Before juicing citrus fruits, cut and reserve about 6 thin slices each of lemon and lime for garnish.

Combine lemon juice, lime juice, sugar, and water in a 2-quart pitcher. Stir until sugar is completely dissolved. Add raspberries, cover, and chill overnight.

Add lemon and lime slices and stir well before serving. Pour over ice.

Cucumber Mint Cooler
Serves 8-10

This fragrant flavored water cools the body from the inside out on even the hottest of Summer days. Make a batch a day ahead and allow it to rest for 8 hours to develop the best flavor.

> **6 cups water**
> **¼ cup fresh mint leaves, bruised**
> **1 small cucumber, sliced**
> **1 cup honeydew melon, cut into chunks**
> **¾ cup sugar**

Combine all ingredients in a 2-quart pitcher. Stir until sugar is completely dissolved. Cover and refrigerate for 4 hours for a lighter flavor or up to 8 hours for a more pronounced flavor.
Stir well and strain mixture, discarding solids. Serve over ice.

Arugula Salad with Berry Dressing
Serves 4

Sweet strawberries and blackberries bring an unexpected Summer flavor to this light and crisp salad!

1 cup strawberries, hulled and halved
2 Tbsp. balsamic vinegar
1 Tbsp. canola oil
1 tsp. honey
Dash of salt
1 4-oz. log goat cheese (chevre)
4 cups arugula leaves
¾ cup blackberries

For berry dressing, in blender container combine 3/4 cup strawberries, vinegar, oil, honey, and salt. Cover and blend until smooth. Set aside. Slice goat cheese crosswise into 8 slices.

Place arugula and remaining strawberries in serving dish. Top with blackberries and cheese slices. Drizzle with berry dressing. Serve at room temperature or chilled.

Yellow Peppers with Tomatoes and Gorgonzola Cheese

Serves 4-6

Grilled peppers bring a smoky sweetness to this quick, easy, and hearty salad.

> 2 Tbsp. olive oil
> 2 Tbsp. balsamic vinegar
> 1 Tbsp. green onions, finely chopped
> 1 Tbsp. fresh basil leaves, finely sliced
> 1 tsp. sugar
> ½ tsp. Dijon mustard
> black pepper to taste
> 3 large yellow bell peppers, sliced into rings
> 3 large tomatoes, sliced into wedges
> 5 cups baby spinach leaves or other salad greens
> 2/3 cup (about 3 oz.) crumbled Gorgonzola cheese

For the dressing, combine the olive oil, vinegar, green onions, basil, sugar, and Dijon mustard in a jar. Cover and shake to blend. Add black pepper to taste. Chill for up to 24 hours.

Roast pepper rings on the grill or on an oiled sheet pan under the broiler for 5 to 6 minutes, until they are just tender, turning once halfway through cooking.

Divide spinach or salad greens equally among serving plates and top each with several tomato wedges and pepper rings. Sprinkle with crumbled Gorgonzola and drizzle with prepared dressing. Serve immediately.

Roasted Corn & Wild Rice Salad
Serves 4-6

This salad is a favorite on our family picnics. All of the vibrant colors and flavors of the season come together in this festive dish. It is best made ahead and allowed to rest.

½ cup uncooked wild rice
1 ½ cups fresh whole kernel corn (about 3 ears)
½ cup tomato, seeded and diced
½ cup yellow or green bell pepper, finely chopped
1/3 cup minced fresh cilantro
2 Tbsp. jalapeno peppers, seeded and minced
2 Tbsp. fresh lime juice
2 Tbsp. prepared honey mustard
1 Tbsp. olive oil
½ tsp. ground cumin

Place 1 ½ cups water in a saucepan and bring to a boil over high heat. Stir in wild rice; cover. Reduce heat to low and allow rice to simmer for about 40 minutes, until it is just tender but still firm to the bite. Drain rice and set aside.

Preheat oven to 400°F. Spray a baking sheet with nonstick cooking spray or brush with butter. Spread corn kernels evenly over prepared baking sheet. Bake for 20 to 25 minutes or until corn is lightly browned, stirring after about 10 minutes.

Combine rice, corn, tomato, bell pepper, cilantro, and jalapenos in a large bowl. Whisk together lime juice, honey mustard, oil, and cumin in a small bowl until well blended. Drizzle over rice and corn mixture and toss to coat. Cover and refrigerate for at least 2 hours. Serve cold and on lettuce leaves, if desired.

Mozzarella & Tomato with Lemon Dijon
Serves 4-6

The tangy bite of lemon and mustard make the fresh flavors of summer tomatoes and basil pop in this salad. Velvety mozzarella balances out the dish.

> 1/3 cup olive oil
> ¼ cup Dijon mustard
> 2 Tbsp. lemon juice
> 2 Tbsp. fresh basil leaves, finely chopped
> ½ tsp. sugar
> 3 medium tomatoes, sliced
> 6 oz. fresh mozzarella cheese, sliced
> 2 cups mixed salad greens
> ¼ cup calamata olives, pitted and finely chopped

In a small bowl, whisk together oil, mustard, lemon juice, basil, and sugar; set aside. Arrange tomato and cheese slices over salad greens on serving plates or a platter. Top with chopped olives and drizzle with prepared dressing. Serve slightly chilled.

Roasted Eggplant and Red Pepper Sandwich Spread

Serves 6-8

Even the tiniest garden can yield more eggplant than a family can handle for a season. Try this recipe for a wholesome, everyday sandwich filling that will leave none of your bumper crop to wither!

1 medium eggplant, split lengthwise
1 large red bell pepper, seeded and quartered
1 bulb garlic
2 Tbsp. fresh oregano, finely sliced
1 Tbsp. tomato paste
1 Tbsp. white wine vinegar
1 tsp. olive oil
salt and pepper to taste

Preheat oven to 425°F. Place eggplant and red pepper skin sides down on an oiled baking sheet. Cut off the sprout end of the garlic bulb, exposing the end of each clove, and wrap completely in foil being sure to leave the cut end facing up. Place on baking sheet. Roast vegetables for 25 to 30 minutes, or until eggplant is softened and pepper skins are blistered and dark. Allow to cool for 15 minutes.

Scoop softened flesh from eggplants with a spoon and place in a blender or food processor. Remove and discard pepper skins. Add pepper flesh to eggplant. Remove softened garlic cloves from cut end of the bulb and place in blender. Pulse until the mixture is coarsely chopped. Add oregano, tomato paste, vinegar, and olive oil, blending until all ingredients are smooth. Season with salt and pepper to taste.

Place in a tightly covered container and refrigerate for up to three days. Serve warm or cold.

Cool and Crunchy Veggie Sandwich Filling
Serves 6-8

This chunky filling is delicious tucked into a pita with fresh sprouts and thinly sliced apple. It makes a great alternative to egg or chicken salad for your next picnic!

8 oz. package cream cheese, softened
¼ cup celery, finely chopped
¼ cup carrot, shredded
2 Tbsp. sunflower kernels
1-2 Tbsp. milk

In a large bowl, combine cream cheese, celery, carrot, and sunflower kernels. Stir until blended. Add milk until mixture is smooth and easy to spread.

Place in a tightly covered container and refrigerate for up to three days. Serve cold.

Nutty Cucumber Sandwiches
Serves 4-6

This hearty and flavorful sandwich makes a terrific light supper on those hot Summer evenings when you just can't bring yourself to cook.

> **8 thin slices rye bread**
> **½ cup snow pea pods, trimmed**
> **3 – 4 oz. goat cheese (chevre)**
> **1/3 cup seasoned roasted soy nuts**
> **1 small cucumber, peeled and thinly sliced**
> **1 medium tomato, thinly sliced**

Steam snow pea pods for 1 or 2 minutes until they are tender-crisp. Rinse under cold water and pat dry.

Spread one side of each slice of bread with goat cheese and sprinkle with soy nuts, pressing them lightly into the cheese. Top four slices with cucumber, tomato, and snow pea pods. Finish with remaining bread slices. Serve immediately.

Spicy Radish and Herb Croissant Sandwiches
Serves 6-8

Horseradish adds a welcome bite to these quick and easy sandwiches on flaky croissants. Wake up your taste buds and try them for brunch!

2 5-oz. containers cream cheese with garlic and herbs
8 croissants, split
6-8 tsp. hot-style prepared horseradish
2 Tbsp. green onion, finely chopped
1 large cucumber, very thinly sliced
10-12 radishes, very thinly sliced

In a medium bowl, combine cream cheese, horseradish, and green onion, stirring until very well blended.

Spread the cut sides of each croissant half with about 1 ½ tablespoons of the cheese mixture. On the bottom croissant pieces, arrange cucumber and radish slices. Complete each sandwich with the top half of the croissant. Serve immediately.

Easy Zucchini and Tomato Bake
Serves 6-8

This dish can serve as a delicious side or take center stage as the main course. The combination of zucchini and tomato is a Summer standard!

> 3 medium zucchini, sliced into ½ inch disks
> 2 medium tomatoes, cut into ½ inch thick slices
> 1 medium green bell pepper, seeded and chopped
> ½ cup onion, finely chopped
> ½ tsp. salt, or to taste
> 1/8 tsp. freshly ground black pepper
> ½ tsp. dried basil
> ¼ cup olive oil
> 2 Tbsp. grated Parmesan cheese

Preheat oven to 350°F. Arrange zucchini and tomatoes, alternating and slightly overlapping slices, in a 1 ½ quart oiled baking dish. Sprinkle chopped peppers, onion, salt, pepper, and basil evenly over the top. Drizzle with olive oil and bake, uncovered, for 25 minutes or until the zucchini is just tender.

Top with grated Parmesan cheese and serve hot.

Southern Style Summer Squash Casserole
Serves 4-6

Try this recipe for a wholesome and different way to use all of the garden's overwhelming squash yield. What makes it southern? Why, butter, of course!

> **2 pounds yellow squash, sliced**
> **¼ cup butter**
> **6 green onions, finely chopped; reserve one half**
> **½ cup chopped celery**
> **2 thick slices French bread, torn in small pieces**
> **½ cup milk**
> **1 to 2 tsp. sugar**
> **2 Tbsp. butter, cut in small pieces**
> **¼ cup bread crumbs**

Preheat oven to 350°F.

Boil squash in lightly salted water until tender. Drain. Melt butter in large saucepan; add all but half of the chopped green onion tops and the chopped celery. Sauté until tender.

Soak bread in milk, gently squeeze out excess milk. Add bread, squash, sugar, and remaining onion tops. Blend well.

Pour into a 7 x 11-inch baking dish. Dot top with butter and sprinkle with bread crumbs. Bake for 20 to 25 minutes, or until crumbs are brown.

Zesty Eggplant Patties
Serves 4-6

The hefty fruits of the eggplant are a fitting symbol for Nature's fertility this season. These tasty patties are wonderful as a side dish along with sliced tomatoes or a little fresh salsa.

1 cup eggplant, diced & boiled until tender
¾ cup cooked rice
1 egg
3 Tbsp. flour
¼ tsp. ground cumin
¼ tsp. ground cayenne pepper
2 Tbsp. onion, finely chopped
1/2 cup sharp Cheddar cheese, shredded
½ teaspoon salt
black pepper to taste

Drain eggplant. Combine all ingredients in a large bowl, mixing well. Cover and chill for 30 minutes to an hour.

Warm 2-3 tablespoons vegetable oil in a non-stick skillet over medium-high heat. Add eggplant mixture, 2 tablespoons at a time, to the skillet and flatten with the back of an oiled spatula. Fry for 3-4 minutes on each side, or until slightly crisp and golden brown.

Serve hot.

Zucchini with Sweet Peppers and Feta Cheese
Serves 4-6

This delicious, quick, and easy dish will quickly become a summertime favorite. It definitely makes cooking in the heat of the season worthwhile!

> **1 cup onion, finely chopped**
> **1 Tbsp. olive oil**
> **3 medium zucchini, cut into 1/4-inch slices (about 4 cups)**
> **2 Tbsp. water**
> **½ teaspoon ground cumin**
> **½ cup bottled roasted red sweet peppers, drained and cut into strips**
> **Salt and pepper to taste**
> **2 Tbsp. crumbled feta cheese**

In a large skillet, sauté onion in hot oil over medium heat for 5 minutes or until tender. Add zucchini, water, and cumin to skillet; reduce heat. Simmer, covered, for 3 to 5 minutes or until zucchini is just tender.

Stir roasted pepper strips into zucchini mixture; heat through. Season to taste with salt and pepper. Sprinkle with feta cheese and serve immediately.

Linguini with Mushrooms
Serves 4

Aromatic herbs take this dish from creamy and comforting to fresh and delicious. Feel free to substitute your favorite summertime mushrooms for the white buttons.

4 cups cooked linguini, prepared according to package directions
3 Tbsp. butter
1 Tbsp. olive oil
½ cup onion, finely chopped
3 cloves garlic, minced
12 oz. fresh button mushrooms, halved or quartered
1 Tbsp. fresh thyme, leaves pulled from stems
1 Tbsp. fresh Italian flat leaf parsley, chopped
½ cup heavy cream
½ cup grated Parmesan cheese
½ tsp. salt
¼ tsp. black pepper

In a large skillet, heat butter and oil over medium heat. Add onion and cook until tender. Stir in mushrooms, garlic, thyme, parsley, salt, and pepper. Cook 4-5 minutes or until mushrooms are slightly browned.

Add cream to mushroom and herb mixture. Bring to a soft boil and then reduce heat. Simmer for 2-3 minutes until thickened and stir in Parmesan cheese.

Divide warm linguini onto serving plates or arrange on a platter. Spoon sauce over pasta and sprinkle with additional thyme or Parmesan cheese, if desired. Serve hot.

Pearl Onions with Pasta Nests

Serves 4

Sweet and delicious browned onions rest in tangles of angel hair pasta to represent eggs in a nest – perfect for celebrating the fertility of the season at your dining table.

1 Tbsp. butter
1 Tbsp. olive oil
2 lb. pearl onions
½ tsp. salt
¼ tsp. ground black pepper
4 oz. dried coiled angel hair pasta
1 ¼ cups water

In a large skillet, heat butter and olive oil over medium heat until butter melts. Add onions, salt, and pepper. Cook, covered, for 15 minutes, stirring occasionally. Uncover. Cook for 10 to 15 minutes more or until onions are tender and browned, stirring frequently. Remove onions from skillet; set aside.

Add pasta to hot skillet. Cook and stir for 4 minutes or until pasta is browned. Add cooked onions and water to skillet. Bring to boiling; reduce heat. Cover and cook 5 minutes. Uncover. Cook for 3 to 4 minutes more or until pasta is tender, stirring occasionally. Serve hot.

Parmesan-Cornmeal Pancakes
Serves 4-6

These savory and delicate pancakes make a delicious main course for breakfast or brunch and can even serve as an unusual side dish with your evening meal.

> 1 cup all-purpose flour
> ¾ cup yellow cornmeal
> 1/3 cup grated Parmesan cheese
> 1 Tbsp. sugar (optional)
> 1 tsp. baking soda
> ½ tsp. salt
> 1 ¾ cups buttermilk
> 2 eggs, lightly beaten
> 2 Tbsp. cooking oil
> 1/3 cup green onion, finely chopped

In a large bowl, combine flour and other dry ingredients. In second bowl, whisk together remaining ingredients. Stir buttermilk mixture into flour mixture until slightly lumpy, being careful not to over-mix.

Heat a lightly greased griddle or heavy skillet over medium heat. For each pancake, pour 1/4 cup batter onto griddle. Cook until golden; turn when tops are bubbly and edges are slightly dry (1 to 2 minutes per side).

Serve warm with a dollop of sour cream, if desired.

Easy Cornbread with Dried Tomatoes
Serves 6-8

Cornbread mix makes this a fast bread for snacking or as an accompaniment to salads or soups.

> 1/3 cup bulgur or cracked wheat
> ¼ cup sundried tomato pieces
> 1 ½ cups boiling water
> ¼ cup toasted wheat germ
> 1 8-1/2 ounce package corn muffin mix
> 1/4 cup grated Parmesan cheese

Preheat oven to 350°F. In a medium bowl combine bulgur or cracked wheat and tomato pieces. Pour the boiling water over bulgur mixture. Let stand for 5 minutes. Drain well.

Meanwhile, grease an 8x8x2-inch baking pan; sprinkle bottom of pan with half of the wheat germ.

Prepare corn muffin mix according to package directions for corn bread. Stir drained bulgur and tomato mixture into batter along with the Parmesan cheese. Spread in prepared pan. Sprinkle with remaining wheat germ. Bake for 20 to 25 minutes or until a toothpick inserted in center comes out clean.

Hearty Oat and Grain Bread
Serves 10-12

This wholesome bread showcases two of late Summer's golden grains, wheat and oats. Try a slice drizzled with honey from a local farm.

> **2 cups water**
> **1/3 cup cracked wheat**
> **2 Tbsp. cooking oil**
> **2 Tbsp. molasses**
> **1 package active dry yeast**
> **1 cup rolled oats**
> **¼ cup nonfat dry milk powder**
> **¼ cup oat bran or toasted wheat germ**
> **1 teaspoon salt**
> **1 ½ cups whole wheat flour**
> **1 ½ to 2 cups all-purpose flour**
> **Water**
> **1 Tbsp. rolled oats**

In a small saucepan, bring the 2 cups water to a boil; add cracked wheat. Reduce heat. Cover and simmer for 5 minutes. Remove from heat; transfer mixture to a large bowl. Stir in oil and molasses. Cool to lukewarm (105°F to 115°F). Stir in yeast until dissolved. Add the 1 cup rolled oats, the dry milk powder, oat bran or wheat germ, and salt.

Using a wooden spoon, stir in the whole wheat flour; stir in as much of the all-purpose flour as you can. Turn out onto a lightly floured surface. Knead in enough of the remaining all-purpose flour to make a moderately stiff dough that is smooth and elastic (6 to 8 minutes total). Shape into a ball. Place in a lightly greased bowl, turning once to grease surface. Cover and let rise in a warm place until double in size (about 1 hour).

Punch down dough; cover and let rest for 10 minutes. Meanwhile, grease a baking sheet; Shape dough into an 8-inch round loaf; place on baking sheet. Cover and let rise in a warm place until nearly double in size (30 to 45 minutes).

Preheat oven to 375°F. Make 3 diagonal shallow slits across the top of the loaf. Brush lightly with water; sprinkle with the 1 tablespoon rolled oats. Bake for 30 to 35 minutes or until loaf sounds hollow when tapped.

Wild Rice and Oat Bran Bread
Serves 10-12

The toasty flavor of wild rice in this bread helps it pair well with both sweet and savory toppings. Apple butter makes a delicious companion to this loaf.

> 1 ¼ to 1 ¾ cups bread flour
> 1 package active dry yeast
> 1 cup fat-free milk
> 2 Tbsp. honey
> 2 Tbsp. butter or shortening
> ¾ tsp. salt
> 1 cup whole wheat flour
> ¾ cup cooked wild rice, drained and cooled
> 1/3 cup oat bran

In a large bowl, stir together 1 cup of the bread flour and the yeast; set aside. In a medium saucepan heat and stir milk, honey, butter, and salt just until warm (120°F to 130°F) and butter is almost melted. Add the milk mixture on low speed for 30 seconds, scraping bowl constantly. Beat on high speed for 3 minutes. Using a wooden spoon, stir in whole wheat flour, wild rice, oat bran, and as much of remaining bread flour as you can.

Turn out onto a lightly floured surface. Knead in enough of the remaining bread flour to make a moderately stiff dough that is smooth and elastic (6 to 8 minutes total). Shape dough into a ball. Place in a lightly greased bowl; turn once to grease the surface. Cover and let rise in a warm place until double in size (1 to 1-1/4 hours).

Punch down dough. Turn out onto a lightly floured surface. Cover and let rest for 10 minutes. Coat an 8x8x2-inch loaf pan with cooking spray; set aside.

Shape dough into a loaf by patting or rolling. To shape by patting, gently pat and pinch dough into a loaf shape, tucking edges beneath. To shape by rolling, on a lightly floured surface, roll dough into a 12x8-inch rectangle. Roll up, starting from a short side. Seal seams with fingertips as you roll.

Place shaped dough in prepared pan. Cover; let rise in a warm place until nearly double in size (30 to 45 minutes). Preheat oven to 375°F.

Bake about 35 to 40 minutes, or until bread sounds hollow when tapped. If necessary, cover loosely with foil the last 10 minutes to prevent overbrowning. Remove from pan. Cool on a wire rack.

Autumn's Folly

The changing colors of Autumn set the stage for celebration and provide a natural decoration for festivals of remembrance and thanks. Sweet golden corn, ruby red apples, plump orange pumpkins, and rich brown seeds and nuts are like confetti on our tables this season.

Your body feels Winter's steady approach and naturally increases the appetite on Autumn's chilly evenings and crisp mornings. Foods this season take on more hearty properties and nourish the soul every bit as much as they do the body. Cooling dishes make way for heady, spicy dishes that warm. Soups make their return to the menu and share the table with salads reminiscent of Summer.

As the days grow shorter and the nights longer, rejoice in the season with recipes that celebrate the night and the moon.

Fruit and Nut Cabbage Slaw
Serves 8-10

This crunchy salad is both refreshing and filling. It makes a great companion to nearly any menu.

> 4 cups cabbage, shredded or very finely sliced
> 2 cups coarsely chopped pecans, toasted
> 1 ½ cups mixed dried fruit bits
> 1 8-oz. package crumbled blue cheese
> 2 8-oz. containers vanilla yogurt
> 2 Tbsp. honey
> 1 tsp. salt

In a very large mixing bowl, toss together the cabbage, pecans, fruit bits, and blue cheese. Cover and chill until ready to serve (up to 24 hours).

In a medium mixing bowl, stir together the yogurt, honey, and salt. Cover and chill until ready to serve. To serve, add yogurt mixture to cabbage mixture and toss to coat.

Barley, Butternut, and Black Bean Salad

Serves 4-6

This versatile grain and bean salad spotlights Butternut squash just as they are beginning to come into season. This dish is perfect for a lazy weekend lunch!

> 1 cup pearl barley, cooked according to package directions and drained
> 4 Tbsp. olive oil
> 1 cup onion, finely diced
> 2 cups Butternut squash, cubed
> ¼ cup water
> 3 Tbsp. dried parsley
> ½ tsp. salt
> 1 Tbsp. lemon juice
> 2 cups canned black beans, drained and rinsed

In a large skillet, sauté onion and squash in olive oil until the squash is just fork-tender. Add the water and parsley and continue to cook for an additional 2-3 minutes until the squash has softened.

Transfer squash and onion mixture to a large bowl and add remaining ingredients. Toss until well blended. Serve warm or cover and refrigerate to serve cold.

White Bean and Pumpkin Soup
Serves 4-6

Warm and earthy sage brings a comforting quality to this creamy soup. It is so quick and easy that it'll leave you plenty of time to cozy up by the fire.

> **1 15-oz. can pumpkin or 2 cups cooked and mashed fresh pumpkin**
> **1 14-oz. can unsweetened coconut milk**
> **1 15-oz. can cannellini (white kidney) beans, drained and rinsed**
> **2 cups vegetable broth**
> **1 tsp. dried leaf sage, crushed**
> **Salt and pepper to taste**

In medium saucepan, combine pumpkin, unsweetened coconut milk, beans, broth, and sage. Heat through. Season to taste with salt and pepper.

Persian Lentil Stew
Serves 8-10

Spicy and delicious! This stew elevates the lentil from mundane to magnificent!

½ cup green lentils
¼ cup dried Split Peas
¼ cup red Lentils
1 cup onion, finely chopped
1 lb. frozen Spinach, thawed and chopped
1 cup carrots, finely chopped
1 large Tomato, chopped
2 fresh green chilies, split
6 cups water
2 Tbsp. olive oil
5 cloves garlic, minced
1 Tbsp. grated fresh ginger root
1 Tbsp. ground coriander
1 tsp. salt
½ tsp. cayenne
½ tsp. cinnamon
½ tsp. ground cloves
¼ tsp. turmeric
½ cup water

Combine lentils, peas, 6 cups water, 1/2 of onion, spinach, carrots, tomato, and chilies in large pot. Heat to boiling and simmer for 15-20 minutes.

In a large skillet, sauté remaining onions, garlic and ginger until golden brown. Add spices and sauté for 30 seconds until fragrant. Deglaze with 1/2 cup water and bring to boil.

Add garlic spice mixture to lentils and simmer, uncovered, for 15 minutes. Serve hot.

Smoky Autumn Night Soup
Serves 4-6

This super-easy soup requires really no prep time and the results are filling and flavorful. Try the cinnamon if you are feeling adventurous – it is a surprisingly good accompaniment to tomatoes.

> **1 28 oz. can diced tomatoes**
> **1 15 oz. can black beans, drained and rinsed**
> **1 15 oz. can pumpkin**
> **½ tsp. ground coriander**
> **½ tsp. ground cumin**
> **1 tsp. cinnamon (optional)**
> **1 tsp. salt**
> **2 cups water**

Combine all ingredients in a large pot and bring to a slow boil. For a creamier soup, remove from heat and stir in ¾ cup half-and-half. Serve hot.

Wild Rice Soup
Serves 6-8

Hearty, colorful, and creamy – the perfect soup for lazy autumn evenings. This dish makes a tasty accompaniment to the classic grilled cheese sandwich.

3 cups water
1 14-oz. can vegetable broth
1 10-oz package frozen mixed vegetables
1 6-oz. package long grain wild rice blend
1 cup milk
½ cup lentils
½ cup American cheese, cut into small pieces

Rinse and sort lentils, discarding any debris or blemished lentils. Combine lentils and water in a small saucepan. Bring to a boil; reduce heat to low and simmer, covered, for 5 minutes. Let stand, covered, for about 1 hour. Drain and rinse lentils.

Cook rice according to package directions in a medium saucepan. Add lentils and remaining ingredients. Bring to a boil; reduce heat to low and simmer, uncovered, for about 20 minutes.

Serve hot.

Baked Rice with Fruit and Nuts
Serves 4-6

This sweet and savory dish combines many of the season's best flavors. Try it as a side this Thanksgiving in place of your traditional dressing!

>**2 cups hot water**
>**1 cup chopped apple**
>**¾ cup long grain rice**
>**¼ cup green onion, finely chopped**
>**¼ cup dried cranberries or raisins**
>**¼ cup toasted slivered almonds, sunflower nuts, or pine nuts**
>**1 ½ Tbsp. butter**
>**2 tsp. instant chicken-flavor bouillon granules**
>**½ tsp. Chinese Five-Spice powder**

Preheat oven to 350°F. In a 2-quart baking dish, combine water, apple, uncooked rice, green onion, dried fruit bits or raisins, almonds, butter, bouillon granules, and five-spice powder.

Bake, covered, for 30 to 35 minutes or until rice is tender. Serve warm.

Golden Corn Pudding

Serves 4-6

Here is a quick and easy take on a crowd-pleasing classic!

2 cups corn kernels
2 cups whole milk
2 Tbsp. cornstarch
½ cup sugar
1 tsp. salt
2 eggs
1 Tbsp. butter

Preheat oven to 350°F. Pour corn into a 2-quart baking dish. Add sugar and eggs, blending well. In a separate bowl, whisk together milk, cornstarch, and salt. Stir into corn mixture. Dot with butter and bake for 45 minutes, or until the top is evenly browned. Serve warm.

Fancy Southern Succotash
Serves 4-6

This dressed-up version of succotash is colorful and festive. Smoky chipotle adds a warming flavor to the palette on these cooling days and nights. Try this with rice for a simple main course.

> **1 onion, finely chopped**
> **2 Tbsp. olive oil**
> **1 orange pepper, chopped**
> **2 cups okra, sliced**
> **1 15-oz. can diced tomatoes**
> **1 ½ cup shelled edamame**
> **2 cups corn kernels**
> **2 tsp. garlic**
> **½ tsp. chipotle powder**

In a large skillet, sauté onion in olive oil over medium high heat until translucent. Add chopped pepper and cook an additional 4-5 minutes. Add garlic and okra. Reduce heat to low and stir okra mixture constantly to prevent it from becoming too sticky. When the okra begins to brown, add tomatoes, edamame, corn, and chipotle powder. Simmer until okra and edamame are just tender. Serve hot.

Sweet Potato and Black Bean Burritos
Serves 6-8

Sweet potatoes and black beans together in a tortilla are a perfect marriage of Autumn flavors. Make plenty so you can wrap them individually in foil, refrigerate, and keep them on hand for a quick meal on busy evenings.

6-8 burrito size tortillas
2 large sweet potatoes, peeled, diced, and boiled until tender
2 oz. cream cheese
2 cups canned black beans, drained and rinsed
1 cup onion, finely chopped
1 garlic clove, minced
1 Tbsp. olive oil
1 tsp. salt
1 tsp. cumin
½ tsp. chipotle
½ cup water or vegetable broth
1 cup cheddar or Monterey Jack cheese, shredded
½ cup sour cream

Drain cooked sweet potatoes and return to pan. Mash well with a potato masher or whisk. Stir in cream cheese, salt, and chipotle powder, blending well until cheese is thoroughly incorporated.

In a medium saucepan, sauté onion in olive oil until translucent. Add garlic, cumin, black beans, and water or broth. Simmer for 4-5 minutes for flavors to meld.

On each tortilla, place about ½ cup mashed sweet potato and ½ cup black beans. Top with shredded cheese and a dollop of sour cream. Wrap and serve warm with a side of rice or corn.

Baked Spiced Squash
Serves 6-8

This light and fluffy dish is similar to sweet potato soufflé. Even those who don't normally request squash will be asking for seconds!

2-12 oz. packages frozen cooked winter squash, thawed (or prepare your own to equal 3 cups)
2 egg whites, lightly beaten
¼ cup brown sugar
2 tsp. butter, melted
1 tsp. cinnamon
½ cup herbed croutons, coarsely crushed

Preheat oven to 400°F. Combine squash, egg whites, sugar, butter, and cinnamon, mixing well. Pour into a 1-quart baking dish sprayed with nonstick cooking spray or rubbed lightly with oil.

Bake 20-25 minutes or until center is set. Remove from oven and sprinkle the top with crushed croutons. Return dish to oven and bake an additional 5-7 minutes or until croutons are browned.

Serve warm.

Sicilian Caponata
Serves 4-6

If you garden then you know that eggplant are prolific producers and will offer their fruits well into October and November in moderate climates. This Sicilian classic is a great way to keep your garden's late harvest from going to waste.

1 ½ pounds unpeeled eggplant, cut into ½ inch cubes
2 ½ cups sliced onion
1 ¾ cups (14.5 oz can) Italian seasoned diced tomatoes, undrained
1 cup chopped celery
1/3 cup chopped ripe olives
¼ cup balsamic vinegar
5 Tbsp. olive oil
2 Tbsp. capers
2 tsp. sugar
½ tsp. salt
Black pepper to taste

Heat 3 Tablespoons olive oil in a medium skillet over high heat. Add eggplant; cook for 6 minutes or until eggplant is tender. Remove from skillet and drain on paper towels.

Add remaining 2 Tablespoons olive oil to skillet and heat over medium. Sauté onions and celery for 5 minutes or until tender. Stir in tomatoes (with juice) and eggplant. Bring the mixture to a boil. Reduce heat and simmer, covered, for 15 minutes. Stir in olives, vinegar, capers, sugar, salt, and pepper and cook an additional 5 minutes.

Serve hot.

Tex-Mex Barley Bake
Serves 6-8

A simple but hearty grain combines with pinto beans and Mexican inspired spices for a one-dish meal that is bursting with flavor.

- 3 cups cooked pinto beans
- 2 cups cooked pearl barley
- 1 15-oz. can Mexican style diced tomatoes, drained
- 1 cup sliced ripe olives
- 1 small onion, chopped
- 1 small green bell pepper, chopped
- 1 cup shredded Cheddar cheese
- 1 Tbsp. olive oil
- 1 clove garlic, chopped
- 1 ½ tsp. chili powder
- ½ tsp. ground cumin
- ½ tsp. salt

Cook and stir onion and green pepper in oil over medium-low heat for about 10 minutes. Add garlic. Stir constantly for about 1 minute. Add remaining ingredients except cheese.

Pour into a lightly oiled 1 ½ quart casserole dish. Bake at 350°F oven for 35 to 40 minutes or until hot and bubbly. Top with cheese. Bake an additional 5 to 10 minutes or until cheese is melted.

Serve warm.

Pumpkin Bread
Makes 2 Loaves

This easy to make quick bread is delicious when sliced, toasted, and topped with a pat of butter. Keep one loaf for yourself and give the second to a friend!

1-14.5oz. can pumpkin
1 ½ cups sugar
½ cup butter, softened
2 large eggs
½ cup milk
1 tsp. vanilla
2 ½ cups all-purpose flour
1 tsp. baking soda
1 tsp. salt
1 tsp. cinnamon
1 tsp. ginger
½ tsp. nutmeg
¼ tsp. cloves

Preheat oven to 350°F. In a large bowl, stir together flour, baking soda, salt, and spices. Set aside.

In a second large bowl, mix sugar, butter, and eggs with an electric mixer. Blend at medium speed for about 1 minute, until slightly fluffy. Add pumpkin, milk, and vanilla. Mix until smooth. Add dry ingredients and mix until just moistened. Avoid over-mixing as it will create a tough bread.

Divide batter into two oiled loaf pans and bake in center of oven for about 75 minutes, or until a toothpick inserted in the middle of each loaf comes out clean. Cool for 5 minutes in pans and then remove loaves, transfer them to a wire rack, and cool completely.

Dutch Apple Cake
Makes 12 Squares

 Apples here in Virginia are at the peak of their season during September and October. Make use of a bountiful harvest by trying this delectable sugarless cake instead of a traditional pie.

> **6 large apples (peeled, cored, & sliced)**
> **1 ½ cups all purpose flour**
> **½ tsp. salt**
> **2 tsp. baking powder**
> **¼ cup butter**
> **1/3 cup milk**
> **1 egg, beaten**

Preheat oven to 425°F.
 Combine dry ingredients in a large bowl. Cut in butter until the mixture resembles corn meal. Add the milk and beaten egg to the mixture and blend well – the dough will be stiff. Pat the dough into a greased 13x9 pan. Top with sliced apples and bake for about 25 minutes.

Apple Brown Betty
Serves 6

This is one of my favorite apple dishes. Brown Betty is like a blend of apple pie and bread pudding and is every bit as delicious as each!

3 cups peeled, cored, & diced apples
2 cups bread crumbs
1 cup brown sugar
¼ cup water
3 Tbsp. lemon juice
2 Tbsp. butter
¼ tsp. cinnamon
¼ tsp. nutmeg
¼ tsp. salt
Pinch cloves
Grated rind of 1 lemon

Preheat oven to 350°F,

Blend sugar, spices, and salt. Arrange 1/3 of the bread crumbs in a greased 8x8 baking dish. Top crumbs with ½ of the diced apples and sprinkle with ½ of the sugar and spice mixture. Repeat the process, finishing with a layer of bread crumbs.

Mix water, lemon juice, and grated rind and pour over the layers. Dot with bits of butter and bake for about 45 minutes.

Serve warm.

COOK'S NOTES

Cook's Notes

Cook's Notes:

Cook's Notes:

INDEX

Apple Brown Betty 92
Arugula Salad with Berry Dressing 54
Baked Rice with Fruit and Nuts 83
Baked Spiced Squash 87
Barley, Butternut, and Black Bean Salad 78
Black Bean, Rice, and Chipotle Stew 16
Butternut Squash and Hazelnut Lasagna 20
Cheddar and Cider Fondue 26
Chestnut Risotto with Butternut Squash 22
Cool and Crunchy Veggie Sandwich Filling 59
Creamy Potato and Onion Soup 15
Cucumber Mint Cooler 53
Deluxe Hot Chocolate 13
Dried Fruit Pudding 27
Dutch Apple Cake 91
Easy Cornbread with Dried Tomatoes 69
Easy Lemon Dill Egg Salad 39
Easy Zucchini and Tomato Bake 62
Fancy Southern Succotash 85
Fig and Nutmeg Coffee Cake 45
Fruit and Nut Cabbage Slaw 77
Golden Corn Pudding 84
Golden Sun Rum Cake 28
Hearty Oat and Grain Bread 70
Hummus Pita Sandwiches 40
Lavender, Mint, and Lemon Infusion 35
Lemon Ginger Infusion 34
Lemon Pepper Penne Primavera 46
Lemonade with Watermelon and Basil 51
Lentil Soup with Spinach 36
Linguini with Mushrooms 66
Mediterranean Couscous Salad 38
Moroccan Potato and Egg Sandwiches 41

Mozzarella & Tomato with Lemon Dijon	57
Mulled Cider	11
Mulled Wine	12
Mushroom and Artichoke Bake	44
Nutty Brown Rice Salad	19
Nutty Cucumber Sandwiches	60
Pad Thai	43
Parmesan-Cornmeal Pancakes	68
Pea Salad with Radishes and Feta Cheese	37
Pearl Onions with Pasta Nests	67
Penne with Asparagus Pesto	42
Persian Lentil Stew	80
Pumpkin Bread	90
Quick and Creamy Curry	17
Raspberry Lime Lemonade	52
Roasted Corn & Wild Rice Salad	56
Roasted Eggplant and Red Pepper	58
Shepherd's Pie with Potato Topping	24
Sicilian Caponata	88
Smoky Autumn Night Soup	81
Southern Style Summer Squash Casserole	63
Spicy Radish and Herb Croissant Sandwiches	61
Spicy Soba Noodles	47
Sweet Potato and Black Bean Burritos	86
Tex-Mex Barley Bake	89
Thyme and Mint Infusion	33
Warm and Sunny Carrot Soup	14
White Bean and Pumpkin Soup	79
Wild Rice and Oat Bran Bread	72
Wild Rice Soup	82
Winter Potato Salad with Snow Peas	18
Yellow Peppers with Tomatoes and Gorgonzola Cheese	55
Zesty Eggplant Patties	64
Zucchini with Sweet Peppers and Feta Cheese	65

www.ingramcontent.com/pod-product-compliance
Lightning Source LLC
Chambersburg PA
CBHW020016050426
42450CB00005B/494